D1233731

# HOW TO LOVE THE WORLD

ELVIRA BASEVICH

[PANK]BOOKS

# HOW TO
# LOVE
# THE WORLD

# ACKNOWLEDGMENTS

Some of the poems included here have previously appeared in publication elsewhere. I would like to acknowledge the following journals and magazines: "A Universal Map of the Womb" in *Hayden's Ferry Review*; "Birds" in *TriQuarterly*; "The First Word" in *The Gettysburg Review*; "Birthday," "The Way I Scream," and "Would You Believe it" in *Blackbird*; "Hegel is Right Again" and "How the Agpar Test is Performed" in *Poached Hare*; "Joseph Brodsky at Queens College" and "A Refugee Comes Home and Wonders How She Got There" in *Women's Studies Quarterly*; "The Plan in 1919" and "This Was a Bad Idea" in *Feminist Wire*; "Why I Can Only Love You the Way You Are Now" in *Word Riot*; and "The Part of Me that's a Jewish Poet" in *Projector Magazine*.

# TABLE OF CONTENTS

## BOOK I. COMING TO AMERICA

## BOOK II. LIFE IN AMERICA

# HOW TO LOVE TO THE WORLD

## INTRODUCTION
(by way of an unsent letter to my mother)

I remember you in different ways. An odd bounty remains when the ones we love fall away from us. From the world. "She's a raving woman, hysterical really," your husband—my father—often said about you, typically adding "and a chink in secret." As if he meant: especially in the dark, where you coo a little to yourself, the Asiatic part of your heart beating slowly—up to god knows what. Likely you too suspected your own intentions and didn't like yourself very much. It would take many conversations with my sisters and a doctoral degree in philosophy before I began to understand what pickaxed at the roots of your soul; from your girlhood in southern Russia, where everyone thought you were very beautiful and yet, for all that, they didn't want you around, to the oceanside bungalow in Brooklyn whose floorboards swelled with liquid garbage and Coca-Cola and tears, as you sat by the window with an infant at your breast and, let's face it, a really quite extravagant litany of Russian curse words on your lips. More often, I remember your regal sadness and, later on, your indifference, as I waved goodbye from the sidewalk when you'd visit me every now and again. I don't know which of these occasions finally left a lump in my throat the size of a turnip, at the exact point where freshly oxygenated blood enters, already feeling somehow used up, with my eyelashes and drops of the River Don stuck in my wet skin. Before my 20th birthday, I began to discern, with no small amount of grief and self-pity, that the first act of the story of my life would be a story about losing you. I arrived into my adult life as though I'd been shipwrecked into it.

As a young woman who bore a great loss too soon and as a poet who if she suffers, prefers to suffer extravagantly, I became obsessed with you. I was determined to map out a new itinerary. I just needed a more sophisticated sense of geography, the terrain of breast milk and border crossings catalogued in the almanac of a wandering, bombed-out family. I could have started with a magnificent rose garden burning in WWII or the white-lace mountains of Kazakhstan. I began instead where I must begin—with you giving birth to me, your first great act of love towards me. For it really was an act of love, not simply a contortion of muscle and a passing of genetic information. Among the flowering ruins of three civilizations, you stood your ground and gave birth to a baby girl. How much you wanted a daughter! And there I was. You called me into the world and I came. I was obedient then. I responded to your will alone. I would gather the sighs that still linger in the walls of a small hospital in Vienna, the scene where we first met, and drop them into my pocket like small change because even if it is not very much I might still need it later.

In order to tell this story fully, though, I have to begin a little earlier. And so, in writing these poems, in part, I retrace your journey as a Jewish-Uyghur refugee, as you wandered out of the Soviet Union with military convoys and unaccompanied children, like grasshoppers jumping out of a page of the bible. On the way to meet god who in 1989 still posted star-struck letters from America, gushing over certain brands of cars, cigarettes, and canned soup. 24 years old, alone, pregnant, and stateless to boot. I began writing this book when I was 24 years old, on my first return to the city of Vienna. The earth was on fire then, as it is now, and there were thousands more women with children in their bellies walking towards St. Stephen's Cathedral. I would wander the streets, singing your favorite songs aloud, making polite conversation with immigrant women who were waiting for the tram, as if you were about to give birth to me all over again. Helping them with their baby carriages, I was caught off guard by my own reflection in the windows of an upscale candy boutique or a second-hand chandelier shop. I was shocked by what of you was there with me in spite of basic physics. This would be our chance to understand each other. For sometimes the writing of poetry is a kind of time travel; and it is always a preparation for love.

Still there is no getting around the fact that you were not there and that you will not read these poems. The day they are printed you will get up and go to work as usual, and, as usual, you will already be very tired before you pass the ugly latticed mailboxes in your apartment building in Brooklyn, interrupting the precocious hissing of a chorus of radiators in a Kings Highway tenement. After living so much life in succession—one day, after another, and then another—perception is the songs you are always singing to yourself anyway, just to pass the time, such that the actual writing and reading of poetry becomes redundant. Before you drop off your first passenger, rattling in your taxi-cab towards Central Park inside a closed circuit bounded by the West Side highway and 5th avenue. I've been watching you make circles inside it for almost thirty years. And yet, I still insist that a splinter of a daydreaming bone broke off from nothing and now here we are, unable to talk to one another. Since the day you met god and he gave you a green card and the address to the local welfare office and Chinese food restaurant, altogether different things have been on your mind, such as the perpetual torment of finding a parking spot for lunch or a bathroom break. Not the revelations of an over-educated daughter who keeps a record of each broken lightbulb that made the world go a little darker and wonders if you still miss bathing in the Black Sea. And to make things worse, I really believe Plato when he says that poetry alone can pull something good and beautiful out of the nothing that we're still getting used to.

I hope you take it on faith, then, that before I did this I tried every which way to make sense of your absence from my life. Just as true on my first try as it is now, love is the only way-out of a no-way-out. And so, I try again. Except this time, after chewing it over for a decade, I have learned that the prospect of failure does not belong to me alone. It belongs to the world. I give it back to the world: I give it back your absence from my life. Not so that it too would grieve—I know it won't—but because I have no other recourse. Because I love you too much to keep it any longer. Now, the world and I can be humiliated in love together.

At the very least, we can use ourselves as an example for other mothers and daughters struggling for a snatch of tenderness and requiring instructions on how to grieve its passing without shame and embarrassment, especially when the passing years keep passing. And it becomes increasingly difficult to count one's losses with ordinary numbers, the same numbers children use to play games in a schoolyard. Poetry might be a preparation for love, but, as Rilke said, we are thrown into the most difficult things unprepared.

Faithfully yours,

with love,

The Author

## PROLOGUE IN FRAGMENTS

"…Now our partnership is dissolved, I feel so peculiar:
      As if I had been on the drunk since I was born
And suddenly now, and for the first time, am cold sober,
      With all my unanswered wishes and unwashed days
Stacked up all around my life; as if through the ages I had dreamed
      About some tremendous journey I was taking,
Sketching imaginary landscapes, chasms, cities,
      Cold walls, hot spaces, wild mouths, defeated backs,
Jotting down fictional notes on secrets overheard
      In theaters and privies, banks and mountains inns,
And now, in my old age, I wake, and this journey really exists,
      And I have to take it, inch by inch,
Alone and on foot, without a cent in my pocket,
      Through a universe where time is not foreshortened,
No animals talk, and there is neither floating nor flying…"

W.H. Auden

"Reader, I want to say, *Don't die.*"

Ada Limón

"Yes, I would like to bring the wide world to you this time. I've begun so late, really only in recent years, to truly love the world that I shall be able to do that now. Out of gratitude, I want to call my book […] '*Amor Mundi.*'"

Hannah Arendt's Letter to Karl Jaspers

# BOOK I. COMING TO AMERICA

INVOCATION OF THE MUSES

O Muse,
lay me down in the cradle of the world.
Sing to me.
I am your baby girl, Mnemosyne.

Tell the tale of heroines,
of the cities that fell of their own accord
or by Mar's cutlass—
embargos on grain, cassava, petroleum,
belching souls to wander the earth, to drown in her oceans
to dream of America, of her kitchen floors
lined with black- and white-checkered linoleum.

Give me the courage to remember all the people
we watched drown in the electric-light oceans on TV.
A ferry to Elysium.

I sink into the silent past,
the seagulls scatter.

I arrange decaying twigs at the ports—
the mirrors of civilization—
and raise my army of hoplites: yellow-cab drivers, washerwomen,
near-sighted librarians, and gas station attendants.
I strike a match
and split the dark, lighting a path
for a caravan of sticky, cola-soaked stars,
the refuse of a summer night.

To be the light that light follows. A homecoming
for the ships of my fleet
in the silence of the morning,
as cities fall,

a young woman rushes forward,
sweat-streaked and pregnant

with love, love, love.

## THE PLAN IN 1919

I could have been the Empress of Russia, if I had tried harder
not to be born in the snowdrifts of a distant colony,

among glittering spruces and herdsmen waiting for their goats
to return from the mountains, as if summoned by a mosque's call to prayer.

From a White's revolver, in honor of Czar Nicholas the II,
my great grandmother took a bullet to the head. As she flung her soul to Allah—

her extraordinary love orphaning a child to save it—the rightful Empress
dozed off under heavy chandeliers that each weighed as much as a human body.

Throwing up the last lights of the ballroom, tributes of sugar
and flour, name-day saints promised to return in a Mark V tank in the springtime.

If I could make an arrangement with them now, maybe I wouldn't mind
so much that the cherry-blossom trees had opened their pinks and yellows,

but could not stop them as they dumped her body into a pile with the others,
so that, later, it would be impossible for you

to talk to a tree or a snowflake without suspecting that she might hear.
If I can just have this morning, on the crosstown bus clutching a bottle of wine,

a sack of oranges and walnuts, so that we might bake something,
our time together might still pass as if we were building a nest and could slip on

the future like a favorite summer dress. I still have plans to liberate your people,
to seduce Ministers of Finance and slit their throats in their sleep.

I'll call you later, after I've returned to my apartment; and you'll ask,
"What are you up to over there?" "Oh, just sitting around thinking about you."

# REMEMBER VIENNA

I've no reason to be here, as I step off
the train platform into goodbying strangers and pigeon feathers.
Toward what I've left of the world,
inside myself, for you.
Carrying poetry books and pamphlets for poetry readings
like rags pulled from the mouth
of a patient, wheeled out of a surgery
performed by memory.

But whose? My heart beats against my ribcage
like a trapped bird or an infant's rattle,
aging forward and backward, simultaneously;
A ticket stub frightens the rooks from the clocktower.
A ticket agent asks her colleague,
'Did you hear something?'
The streets of neighboring cities begin to vanish.

Stephangasse last seen lathed and smiling, wearing a heavy cape of snow.
Gostalle, the site of a new telephone line, not seen since last Thursday
evening, around 7:45pm.

     I smell tar and roses.

     I'm a decorated cosmonaut,
          growing senile in a drafty, seaside resort,
          smiling at my nurses.

     I'm a breath swaddled in a maternity ward
          and can't distinguish my soul rocking shut
          from the feeling of love.

     I'm alone in a crowded street. I'm dis-

     appearing. I'm standing very, very still.

From a tram conductor's booth, you plead with me
in a language I'm slowly forgetting;
the sun stands motionless over its glass reflection.
Something of you still clings to the departing trains
as I do to my own body
or as a mollusk does to an abandoned harbor.

# THE WORLD, A PHILANDERESS

I can still learn how to love the world,
even though she hurts me with her affairs.

      She runs her fingers between the thighs of other pretty girls.
      She turns to me to ask me, in plain English, what do you want?
           Can't you see there's no one here for you?

           I just don't get it.
Even if I'm a stranger in the city of Vienna.
Even if the cosmos were an enormous bank vault
stuffed with as many stars
      as banknotes
destined to glitter someone else's life and make other people happy,
I still need to track down your name and addresses,
I still need to return what belongs to you: my love, my love.

How is it that, suddenly, ordinary objects—a gutted
telephone booth, where you placed a call
and cried a little, a narrow lobby
you had passed, a gaudy flower stand that had astonished you—
prove that a burnt offering of flesh,
the sacrifice of beautiful daughters, is no deposit for great reward?

I won't give up so much without haggling a little first.
I refuse to let eternity begin, again,
with a firstborn crying out in a barnyard.
It's true that under the frosted-glass stare of magi
standing in afterbirth—in the apotheosis
of counted stars—someone asked for your papers.

But I can still move forward
and backward, simultaneously—
I can build a homeland out of train stations
and café tables propped up by folded strips of cardboard.
I can write in peace.

Under the linden trees,
I watch teenagers float on a wreckage of kisses,
pensioners play checkers
and memories that don't belong to anyone
return, one by one, shaking off a little signal,
the more potent for its softness

like the sweetness that gathers in
the smallest, darkest, and most bruised summer strawberry

like a chapter of World History.

      (And I'm comforted that Abraham is still on the mountain
      carrying on to the clear blue sky about the worth of one or two people.
      I consider him an ally and a good friend.)

A hotel room opens in a vista of algae blooms in the Mediterranean.
Bellhops sweep through the water
and blow bubbles with the frowning fish; the sudden repose of sea flowers
quiets a crying baby. Sitting on a plastic crate,
your ghost crushes tobacco leaves under my fingernails

asks me to judge what is left of my love for the world.

      *I will find one good person.*
      *I will bark orders for infants to be cut in half*
and listen for who screams the loudest—
blows the biggest bubble.

*And I will give myself to her.*

A walk through the cities of eastern Europe, 1989 or 2014, conjoined by life's disappointments, which I remember in exact and invented detail. How did I first get here? When did you stop arriving? Is this the here I am looking for? A shoot ripened into flesh from your torn-open girlhood and, stinking horribly, grew kindness and devotion, a cradle for poems, myths, and fevers. Nursing the weeds in the yard of an emergency clinic, I still look out at the world from the vantage point of your bellybutton.

# A UNIVERSAL MAP OF THE WOMB

Vienna suffered the tracery of blue lights
that puffed over the night sky. In the depths of the air-ocean,
a vein of stars swelled against the dark
until I burst into flesh, thudded into my jelly bones.
Carried by the sewer waters of your body like a cheap love song,
I bobbed through side streets & alleyways,
as weightless as a fish caught in a net,
with the stubborn
will to live
of a piece of plastic.
I acquired a flare for life and listened to the world
crack in the summer heat like expensive china.

The waters followed me. Cathedrals, airports, the painted horses
in the public square,
blew apart, flooded with seawater. I arrived early.
I floated on a wreckage of salt and air-blown kisses,
a deckhand waving from the mast
who felt her purpose was good and has returned to her city,
a fisherman hunting in the night by jacklight,
emptied into the cotton-
ball mouth
of July.

A nesting doll of oceans inside oceans
washes up on the rock-reefs of an ever vaster ocean—
It was good to be alive, to climb like a ladder
the days crossed out in
the kitchen calendars of a dead country.
I breathed the sticky grey-blue pearl of my body.

In a McDonald's in Brooklyn, ten years later,
pink with pride, you will tell me that I was born
a perfect 10 on Apgar's scale.
As you pay for our cheeseburgers, you will turn to me and say,
"Now, let's be like normal people."          And I will promise, "*OK*."

So tonight, I follow the weird star of my birth.
I keep my promise. I consider setting fire to St. Stephen's Cathedral
          or I can drive a tank into the national library,
               whisper obscenities to retirees
who ride trams at dusk and glance in my direction over the evening paper.
     I wheel out my last reserves, without purpose,
               like a lead-poisoned sailor
                    whose homeland
is a black cloud guttering in the reptilian part of the brain—
     I too drag discordant objects across the tundra
               that people will later find and wonder,
                    'What was she thinking?'


     I too speak memory, orphaned,
               carried on a current of feces
and milk, that blossoms pointlessly out of nothing
          like the beginning of the world.

May 4th 1989. The volunteers at the relief organization said you should wait out the months before resuming your journey. A Viennese clinic is better than a public hospital in Rome, they said. You stayed in a furnished walk-up apartment. You were out grocery shopping and the narrow street below clamored with the smell of horse shit and roses.

# BIRTHDAY

> «Родила тебя в пустыне
> я не зря.
> Потому что нет в помине
> в ней царя.»[1]
> Joseph Brodsky, "Lullaby"

A warden of the stars released a bit of light.
It arrived in the distant whining of an ambulance,
in the morning's groceries spilled on the floor,
after you carried your body up the stairs all by yourself.

You were screaming among the oranges.
A child slow to learn, I still hardly understand
doorbells or calendars,
a disassembled mechanism where for a moment our breath

died completely, before flaring up again like a lovesick suitor
at the open window of the world.
That was me singing.
What did you make of us among the truant angels?

A new configuration of the eternal and the infinitely sad.
Like moving a table from one corner
of the room to another, except being both Muslims and Jews,
these transitions are more or less impossible to explain.

My soft bones and organs sustained by a few drops of milk
and kindness. Efficient nurses
laid me on a scale, smiled at my sex. For a handful
of shekels, they hired a band of Bacchantes

to beat their chests at the hospital gates
in praise to the generous void
to the woman who delivered the flower of its violence.
I'm just glad someone took down our names.

---

1    "I gave birth to you in a desert / not in vain, / for within its expanse / no
kings reign." (Translated by the author).

On a real piece of paper. Folding it into your pocket,
so that we'd know how to refer
to ourselves later, and the world, what happened.
Nothing was the same in the city of Vienna.

Shapeless, I lied on your chest,
and cried without thinking, inconsolably –
my first lesson on possessing
flesh and a soul simultaneously.

# HOW THE APGAR TEST IS PERFORMED

*If the infant cries well, the respiratory score is 2.*

In the blue bowl of the morning, fresh cut parsley and scallions cried out in the market below. The scissors had already begun to move through the cotton swabs, antiseptic instruments, and the crisp, white bedsheets. The well-oiled machinery of the days grown inside glass jars like white blood cells shored up our strength.

> Was it? a half-opened window pried apart the mother-of-pearl of our conjoined solitude. Was it? in the cutting of the bright pink envelope, the avenues of a ruined body. I opened my mouth as wide as I could. It was the first day of school. *Here.* Alighting for a hiccup and a burp, in my first human voice, you said,
>
> softly,
>
> «Прекрасно.»

*If heart rate is greater than 100 beats per minute, the infant scores 2 for heart rate.*

Knock, knock, a strand of horses, agitated. Then, a dark hallway, carrying the scent of a summer day, a recent rainfall. A corridor split four ways, a mechanism that glues a ballerina to a music box and sets her spinning. Out of habit, I opened the box. There was music. There were so many people. And a note with a folded corner, passed down by all the painted angels in the nursery.     Dimly, then, I

saw the thing-in-itself,          Plato's original form,
                          the Good in everyone.
       When you think about it,     it's all turning out


                    perfect.

*If there is active motion, the infant scores 2 for muscle tone.*

The almanac of '89, fish nested in tree branches, with hurricaned cars, and Soviet writers
living in exile in the East Village. Snow fell from the lamp-posts of our
convalescence.         What a stroke of luck! In the differentia of animal
kingdoms and introductory metaphysics textbooks,     two instances of
the same kind exist     in extended space and counted time,   even in
slightly different modes,             so,           it makes sense when
they put         us
right next to each other.

Your mode and mine     tingling like little bells.

When the prayers of a wandering Jew slipped out of you and moved
through me,         clinging to my viscera,             distinguishing
your soul from mine,

perfectly.

*If there is grimacing and a cough, sneeze, or vigorous cry, the infant scores 2 for reflex*
*irritability.*

What would you have done, Reader? Ovid writes that the water nymphs of
Albula once gathered at the mouths of dead rivers. In the breaking dusk, its
translucence sunk into the moon's dull glass. Somewhere beneath the elevated
trains and the vegetable garbage of Brighton Beach, I learned to sucked it in
with the dumb faith of a televangelist, of a girl in love. I thought that that
summer would last forever. I could hardly stand it, how good it felt. How *right*.

How
*perfect.*

*If the entire body is pink, the infant scores 2 for color.*

Grinding in the pink marble, the shock of mortality. I'm feeling much
better now. I'm not crying anymore. I arrive at the train station and watch the
schoolchildren; some wave, some spit at the passing trains.

# THE WAY I SCREAM

> "I scream the scream of a newborn baby."
> Yehuda Amichai

I am a licked-over bone thrown into a side-street,
with blood still drying inside my bellybutton.
I've the dignity of someone standing next to a garbage can.
When all I want to do is take off my clothes
and sleep with strangers who chance by this walkway,
trees stir with sparrows taking flight, showing me where I must go,
preparing me for something dumb and heroic.
The most ordinary acts of love make me lose my confidence completely:
a child called to the dinner table, a ghost to providence,
still redolent of a place in the world it was loved in,
mostly corn-silk, bugs, and lightening showers
that crash while kissing each other, like a couple arguing in Russian,
who in flinging a dinner plate across the room
are all the more thoroughly pierced by Cupid's arrow.
Among gas lines and stacks of newspaper,
in a train station in Vienna, I first found your handprint on my heart,
a map that would take me to the steppes of Central Asia,
to sleeping-cars suspended over the Volga River like sugar drops
about to fall into the devouring mouth of my love for you
to settlements where a Jew looks at an Arab
and sees herself, and tables are pushed together
and remain covered with tablecloths laid out only on special occasions
that I can see when I close my eyes and call your name
to everywhere other girls lie awake at night
thinking about what is happening to them—and why is it that an ancient loss
can suddenly throw open the shutters of a solitude
passed onto us at birth, without anyone realizing; the following day fits
into my hands like the broken handle of a coffee pot,
burning faintly. Incapable of making a different kind of sound
or stifling my absurd way of loving—*cross my heart*
*and hope to die*—I climb into a taxi-cab and you begin to fall around me,
a few moths milling under a streetlamp.

# GOOD NEWS! THE WORLD IS A BIG TOILET

Part I. Immanuel Kant's Four Models of the World

The philosopher, astounded by the beauty of the world, wonders: why do human beings expect the end of the world at all? And why must it be terrible? By jukebox lights, on a bar napkin, I draw a map of the world. Only in imagining it as a big toilet is it possible for me to believe that it won't come to a terrible end. I also just really need to pee.

i. A Cheap Inn

Cramped, filthy accommodations. The innkeeper charges exorbitant rates. The rain has pushed apart the roof shingles for the milk-grey sky, a nursemaid opening the tiny mouths of the rotting wood, blood-letting the cold. The roof caves in. But it is always overbooked. 'Arriving here on life's journey,' the angel begins, 'you must be prepared to be driven out soon by succeeding boarders.'

ii. A Prison

A brutal warden, in this world, the people are driven from the vast pastures, skies, and oceans; and they begin to grow sick with guilt for being-in-the-world. They thrust their chest toward the watchtower to be pierced like butterfly specimens and hope that the sixth day that built all the animals and named them after the many names of god will never come again—that it will leave them out of it next time.

iii. A Madhouse

In this pasture, good intentions are rewarded with electric shocks, solitary confinement, the amputation of healthy limbs, brain surgeries. 'A packed trunk, Bulgakov's *The Master and Margarita*, and the act of suicide,' the angel explains, 'are the last vestiges of the human personality. It is Abaddon's order.'

iv. A Latrine

And then the angel points to the distant earth, 'There is the toilet of the whole universe,' and relieves itself before flying back to heaven. We must learn to grow here among the residue of its celestial light, digested fruits, floods, and comets, among all the darkness that fertilized the first star and the first paroxysmal beat of the human heart.

Part II. Our House

Is it an oceanside bungalow? Is it built from clay, brick or tarpaulin?
Does it have any windows? Do they face north or south?
Does the ocean spray foam soapsuds to bathe our sleep?
Can I hear seagulls or smell honeysuckle from inside it?
Has the surrounding city been destroyed? Fire-bombed?
Leveled by door-to-door salesmen or Golgotha's stubborn cross?
Will we be happy, here, on earth, in our house?

HAPPINESS

> "...Happiness is the state of a rational being in the
> world in the whole of whose existence everything goes
> according to her wish and will."
>
> Immanuel Kant

An old Jew in Babel's *Red Cavalry* wonders about Paradise:
"I want an International of kind people,
I would like every soul to be given first-category rations.
There, soul, please eat and enjoy life's pleasures."
What kind of rations would you like?
In which establishment would you prefer to pray?
Through the apparatus of the rolled paper
Of the synagogue or the invisible lines of Borges' old age?
In a country whose soil has not known war,
What has demolished your temples?
Set fire to the fields? Frightened the villagers?
Who have you, in secret, cursed under your breath?

A bombed-out wedding hall
collapses as you run and you don't know what awaits
you at the border; a colossal force moves
through you like the mouth
of a newborn searching for a nipple.

But tell me—

for now,
we have a little time to talk
and to get to know each other—

What *is* your pleasure? In the best of all possible worlds,
What world belongs to you? Do you belong to the world?
Are there Jewish people? Muslims?
Do you have a lot of friends? Do you sleep on
the left or the right side of the bed? Do you sleep well?
Are some things best left out of your control?

The moment the teakettle begins to whistle and you,
standing at the lapping blue coil
of its agitated lips, forgive yourself for not loving me,

> *your own soul,*
>             more.

Tell me, what *is* your pleasure?
Tell me because at the approaching border the people
await news of Paradise,
as if it were a letter sent from one war-torn country
to another; and in their dumb illiteracy,
they will gather around you and beg you to read their letters aloud.

LEARNING TO WALK

I unburdened you from the weight of my body.
       Red stamps bled into our portraits
       in the visa application like a bloom of jellyfish.
              Staatsangehörigkeit:        STAATENLOS
              Größe:                     BABY
              Besondere Kennzeichen:     KEINE

A people who will never return to the cities they planted.
       Seditious writers thankful that liberty
              had only cost them the gold fillings in their teeth,
                  one suspicious fall from a balcony,
           a sleigh ride pulled by a troika of dogs
     and bad dreams, alternatively
considering (and reconsidering) suicide or the synagogue.

In the crowded waiting rooms of immigration offices,
a TV played daytime talk shows
       to help us with our problems
       to teach us good English and offer words of advice:
*In America, you must never wear the same shirt two days in a row.*
          *In America, armpits must be*
            *perfumed with deodorant every morning without exception.*
And the outcry over Madonna's '89 music video
       for "Like a Prayer" meant,
       definitely, *In America, remember, Jesus is not Black!*

You were asked to sit on a stool in front of a camera,
to look to your left
       for what would become the only photograph of us taken that year.
       I look at it now as if I were reading the lines
      of an enormous palm that would carry us to Rome

          the way children escort a beetle from one leaf to another.

This is how I learned to speak four languages in coos alone
and you knew that one day I will be a great philosopher.

And a poet, to boot.
That I'll try my hand at love and lose, at first,
and then win and win and win.
When you walked away, my head tucked against your shoulder,
inside you I felt fidelity move like Aeneas' fleet—
in the dusk, the swans still gather the burnt-up ships of our departure.

## FEAR

And then I grew a little frightened.
I was abandoned by my hoplites,
I carried neither arms nor blood-spattered booty,
with only Virgil to steady my will.
I encountered no seer whose intelligence
and devotion inflamed her passion for me.
No prophesy to impregnate the future
with things that haven't happened yet—
but my faith was like an orchid
bound by tiny strings, around which ever larger
blossoms burst and languish,
even if there were no idle Queens
impatient to fall in love with me
and delay my return to Brighton Beach.

WILD DREAMS

I wonder if you daydreamed about ice cream cones
or made conversation with the fruit vendor.
If it bothered you when, out of pity,
he slipped you extra plums or a packet of almonds.

If you looked up at the Ferris Wheel's
swinging wooden cars and held your breath,
considering, briefly—oblivious to the drift
of your thoughts—buying yourself a ticket. Maybe two.

As I teenager, a homeless drunk I had befriended
tried to give me a silver bracelet, made of real silver,
for Christmas, together with the Macy's receipt
to prove he had purchased it (singing on trains in the dead of winter).

I promptly ended the friendship.
I had cost him $50. When he caught up with me,
demanding: who is he, if he can't give a gift, really working for it
like an ordinary man? Turns out that the ordinary

is a carnival mirror. If you approach it from without,
if you pay too much attention, it shatters you
into shards of hideous pink light: this is why a sense of self
is the pure gold baby, the miracle that knocks you out.

On that wooden car, it would have felt good to sit down
and feel the night move,
as the blue whale of the sky glides back home to Almaty.
I wonder how this city would've appeared
to you then, drowning in lightbulbs.

When an ordinary joy comes crashing in,
the world can seem like a drunk wedding party,
a blue shade in Clotho's weaving;
and the man you once loved raises a toast to you,
half-asleep, draped in the early morning light,

      before being thrown out
into the gutter.
          If only.     A spectacular, punch-drunk love
      was there at the last stitch, with a bloodied nose
and torn blazer, smiling from ear-to-ear like an idiot,
ready to walk you home.

To start over properly. It's not enough for me, all these years later,
to open a window and look out of it,
to walk the streets of Rome, Rostov, or Bolshoi Aksu,
to fall in love with everyone I meet,
as if I were climbing a galloping horse and just have to hold on tight.

In a refugee camp in Lebanon,
a journalist writes to me
about families who sleep in tents barnacled with stars.
His kerosene lamp gathers children
in the circle of its light.
He asks them about their wildest dreams
and they each ask him for a bicycle.

         "A *bicycle*," he writes.

# HOW TO LOVE THE WORLD

"For this is a beautiful world."
W.E.B Du Bois

When I ride my bicycle, I see the sky
move over the earth.
The clinics and maternity wards choke with old magazines.
The sky dribbles into the corridors like a shipwreck;
he is insatiable. He clings to the earth,
pinching her nipples, ready to create new worlds.
In the summer heat, he moves through the prairies
of North America, lingers in her rock-reefs,
sets boats adrift in shipyards, rotted with the sea-wind.
As he makes his way downward
to penetrate veins of her melted snow,
he stiffens against giant blossoms of garbage, silver mines,
and the stopped-up sewage system of Mexico City.
He runs his tongue over her spurting oil jacks.
Puts a live coal in his mouth.
An agitated wing of coral begins to climb up
his thigh; breathing heavily, she tightens her innermost coils
but at a critical moment, he falls back; he gets tired.
At Delos' fish bones, in the entrails of remote cities,
an impatient spume rocks
and turns. Butterflies drop dead out of the sky.
In a grotto, among overgrowths of her salt
and pink seaweed, I take my time.
I ask her to close her eyes.
Against my lips, as daylight falls out of the sky
in sticky pearls, she groans, turns over, and finally falls asleep.

# THE FIRST WORD

> "I wish to confess that we were always
> quite undistinguished dishwashers."
> Aimé Césaire

A homesick sailor harbors
among piles of tin cans and rotting vegetables,
cast out from his tribe by an angry father.
A prophet who emerged from a cave
carries a live recording
of Orpheus singing to the shades that burns up
farmsteads and sets the villagers running.
In Yeshiva, the stories, truly, none of them made sense.
And the impression they gave of God—
he didn't seem very preoccupied with how men
plundered grain or bartered their daughters.
I remember that he rested
after arranging stars into arches and galloping horses
built oceans and stocked them with fish
set the moon in the clouds.
During a rainstorm in Galilee, evil was born
without anyone noticing, like the sprouting of a weed
or the least complicated algae.
I don't know how much of this is true.
After all, you had convinced the rabbi to accept $25
a month to take me in and the teachers
assigned *Sesame Street* to the fourth graders.
All the same, I wondered about god's departure.
In his empty bed, countries were collapsing,
welfare checks went unsent,
languages were written from left to right.
Still warm to the touch, the soil-print of his hands
sinks into my pillowcase
falls in snowflakes into the Detroit River.

I forgive you that you had enough
animal warmth for just one, and you passed it between us
like a bottle of vodka between drunks.
I'm not oppressed by the sun rolling
back like a giant eyeball over the countries
that didn't want us. And I forgive you
for growing homesick for a world
I couldn't restore to you, whatever trials a god invented
for me. I'm glad there are no more stalls

bursting with horseshit to clear. No more girls tied to the sides
of a mountain to fall in love with

and marry. Above all, that nothing I do will make this right
because, as it turns out, we both
live just a breath above the stinking ocean,
with memory, the slowest
but most persevering sea monster.

# WHY I CAN ONLY LOVE YOU AS YOU ARE NOW

Something of you is hanging in the air
in the brightly-painted toy boats drifting along a canal
in the measured clangor of a tramcar
in the moon glimmering like a piece of licked candy.
I am close to how you were then,
my head tucked against your breast,
the sun weeping into the rented rooms of Jewish refugees.
Decades yawn between us like the lips
of an open wound, trafficking in the difficult magic
of simply being in the world.
Your body emptied of my life, weary with creation,
returns to me this oyster-grey morning.
I can almost touch you, comfort you,
say something kind to you, but instead dispatch a basket
on an isolated waterway, heavy with the future
and the reflected crowns
of limbless trees, because sometimes abandoned infants
really do return to found a civilization.

# THE SEA MONSTERS OF ITALY

In the narrow throat of Italy,
I sunbathed with one-eyed, fish-tailed Mnemosyne.
She'd grown hideous with age,
strained by my ridiculous will to live.
Whipped by the winds of exile,
even monsters do not want to turn up
swaddled in a basket at the door of a monastery
or in a state-run hospital.
I walked the catacombs,
buried myself in a mountain,
ordered gelato.
Goethe of the dilapidated courtyards.
Calliope, accidentally.
My fingers groped the bellies of lambs—
I clung to them for the love-of-life.
My brothers, the Cyclopes, tried to eat me.
The Titans were neglectful parents.
I've cataloged your sterile mythology, nine daughters,
a ruined world
that hatched a new order of space and time, hung the moon
on a cloud.
A rape that no one prevented
by the turn of a new species of trees
or an insect
or a moo-cow.
Carts and makeshift stalls sell fabrics
and spices to stop the bleeding.
And I too trade in warmth,
as if it were a fish wrapped in a newspaper
but I can't tell: is this your body or mine—?
Am I too a willing spectator?
Watching a beautiful girl of a religious minority being fed to lions.
At the crooked-lipped fountains of Rome,
I'm surprised that I care so much.

I've returned, after all. Here I am, an archer tracking
in the hot snows of a volcano,
at the footfalls of an August night,
the black jetties of the Tyrrhenian sea,
the coast I wandered as a girl,
your life and mine,
the soft lines of the belly, breasts, pubis,
swell with bruises and new fevers. If I were to say to you
that we were worth it,
that doesn't mean that any of this
should happen again
to anyone.

# BOOK II. LIFE IN AMERICA

*How did we fare in the intervening years? With my dumb will to live, turn pink, and cry aloud. Can't complain, I guess. But suppose I could? Suppose I were to protest, scream? It makes no sense to ask you now that you're back in the Soviet Union on the border of Alexander's conquest of the Urals, where it is always 1987 and you are 22 years old forever, the same age I will be when I first fall in love.*

CHRISTMAS IN DETROIT

Some scientists speculate that Amelia Earhart
crashed into an island in the Pacific
and was eaten by giant coconut crabs. That's why
her body was never found. My theory
is that it's the second snowstorm of the month
and everything moonlights as a parking lot here.
The snowed in plain speckled with shrubs
and chain-smoking grates. The island of Nikumaroro
as I imagine it driving through the sleet.
The baseball stadium. A Ford pick-up
parks on the pitcher's mound; the players just run around it.
Even the sky is one big empty parking lot—
drop a quarter in the meter and it will return
as an icy bubble blown so hard
it hurts the skin a little. Amelia Earhart
would've had better luck flying a car
over the Pacific in 1937. That way,
her success would've been even more miraculous
and no one would've been surprised when she goes missing
and is declared dead *in absentia.*
And anyway, who cares about some lunatic
who drives her car into the ocean? I prefer women
who walk into it, Alfonsina Storni,
limp and stony-eyed at Mar del Plata,
forever oblivious to the cold and the love of thousands
of Argentine teenagers. Either way,
in the end, you might still get eaten by giant coconut crabs.
Sometimes there's just no helping that.

# HEGEL IS RIGHT

> "There is nothing degrading about being alive."
> G.W.F. Hegel

From the revelations of a barber's sleep,
    wrapped in rags and coupon clippings,
juts the crooked branch of our bloodline; and this time we are Americans.
We used to wake up in Brooklyn with leaves in our hair.
    Hang the Star of David over
pipes in the wintertime and pretend we bathed in hot water, the way god intended.

Now I'm a big success in this country.
    Like a well-timed birthday cake, a mobster's wife or an aging boxer,
I enter a room and people stop talking for some reason.
    As of a draft mandate,
the average, able-bodied American male is afraid of me.
    I've split in two Césaire's dreadful zero of our reason for living.

On the one side, you're carrying a crying baby,
    a crumbling paperback with a Green Card hidden in the spine.
On the other side, a Miss America contestant asks
    a live audience for world peace,
a living wage, a bungalow by the Atlantic Ocean, and really means it.

## HEGEL IS RIGHT AGAIN

> "[But] the fact that things merely are
> is of no help to them."
> G.W.F. Hegel

I am a cosmonaut and run a real risk of exploding in outer space.
The talismans you gave me were useless
against the violent splendor of galaxies
bubbling in the backs of angels,
growing suns like a new pair of wings.
Useless against keeping my suitors from falling in love with me.
I rip up their letters and grow gloomy
at the sight of the flowers they send me. When I miss you,
at the sound of footfalls in the corridor,
I still shove them into the closet, but it is never you anymore.

More than anything I would like to do something to upset you
but I am a university professor now
and all my friends admire me. For an extra helping of bread
and potatoes, I no longer need to write love letters
to governments anywhere on this bludgeoning
star that shakes off human beings
like breadcrumbs from a tablecloth after Shabbos.

An amphora will show who struck first—
that a peplos and a flower blew in the wind,
when Asia Minor first blushed with riches,
dumb with unrepentant thieves and the murder of civilizations.
When you first raised your voice
to curse god and laughed at the created world
he created, as a still illiterate child,
a poem came to me like a dove with a branch.
I did not know then
that we too were the dove and the branch.

Existence is perfection, you said, my first love,
my medieval philosopher. In compensation for not being born
with a little more money or a nationality—
neither the offspring of providence nor the ocean—
I was born completely naked.
A nurse laid me across your chest
and a demented arrow flew us to America.

GLORY

Under a clothing line crowded with sleeping nightingales,
school children
left flowers with the landlady while we were out,
and when we travelled on,
they piled into train stations to wave goodbye.

With the days of the calendar pressed to our foreheads
like a closed window,
I learned to make peace with the fact
that the will of Joan of Arc
burned together with the clothing on her body.

But on certain nights
a moon slowly climbs out of an old suitcase.
Flicked against a matchbook or an old razor blade,
the moonlight still catches on the curtains,
rising like a staircase in the night.

In the morning, among girls on summer vacation,
bathing in a lake,
I gather the shock of the this-is-what-life-could-be-like feeling.
          I laugh.
I admire our glistening bodies among the cabbage flowers.

Someone will come looking for us eventually,
guided by the rumors of the fishermen and the fish,
with lanterns and a mapmaker;
some will arrive
for the sake of love—and others, for the glory.

# DEMETER'S GONE TO WORK

As eternity rolls along like a beer can
tossed from the window of a speeding truck,

Demeter quits shaking with fury
the reeds that nod along the overpass.

She's tired. She can barely keep
her eyes open to watch as her daughters

are taken and returned.
The month of April comes and goes

as usual and winter never arrives
for all the men who had never deserved

her endless summer. She drags her cart
of days, moving by a reserve of light

that had once broken the will of Olympians,
rained lightning showers,

raised civilizations, and taught men
how to domesticate a herd of wild stars

to begin the age of agriculture.
She did all that for them. She does it still,

except now there are no cults
in her name, no one to placate her godhead

or to listen to her heartache. She leaves at
the break of day to fan poppy seeds

and the giddy bones of windmills
that still move inside her. She packs a turkey sandwich

for lunch. Behind the wheel of a yellow taxi-cab,
she's stuck in traffic with a talkative fare.

In the lobby of an expensive hotel,
she scrubs bubblegum out of a carpet.

In stockrooms, she lines bakeries with fresh rolls.
The markets are crowded with her vegetables.

In the winter that never comes,
poppies shout everywhere the sun breaks

its yoke, her earth's laughter. As she picks up the nightshift,
another fare climbs into the backseat

        and another daughter disappears.
The seaside trembles like the plucked string  of a lyre.

# JOSEPH BRODSKY AT QUEENS COLLEGE (OR, ME AT WORK)

I try to imagine him talking to the secretary
lecturing to his students who must have looked up at him
as they look up at me now, with the heavy-lidded heart of Orpheus,
stuffed with sawed-off branches and the light
of moonscapes, the glint of snails, clay, and mortar shells.
They too only half mean to sing low to themselves,
lift lines from epic poetry and actually conjure something from another world.

How interesting it must have been to catch him in the corridor
on his way to the toilet or just stretching his legs a bit,
to watch his face change expression as he accidentally steps on
a wad of bright pink bubblegum,
tries to drink from defunct water fountains and makes the janitors
sob aloud from the sudden revelation
of the agony of having to love today and again tomorrow.

I'd have enjoyed exchanging cock-and-bull remedies for a chest cold,
ruining his day with a pointless argument,
or just listening to him complain about bus schedules,
the plastic spoons in the cafeteria,
and the old-fashioned timetables of college administrators.
I can only guess whether he was the kind of old bachelor
who gave gifts to girls like a man sitting down

to an out-of-tune piano and who stubbornly keeps playing it.
A dram of vodka. A gunshot to the temple. The last dream
of the morning. The teakettle shapes a winter day into a flying chariot.
Olive oil leaps out of the frying pan,
as his housekeeper sheds a reluctant tear for her days
in the *komsomol*, when the motherland
was victorious and men still looked at her a certain way.

Slipping his feet into dog-eared slippers, he must have
thought to himself—as I did this morning—that it is hard to love
the world and oneself in it, with its arrangement
of flowers and false eyelashes. Its many druggists and dentists

clutching the insides of a subway car. Workers who no longer
bother to strike. Patients getting lost in the halls
of poorly-funded hospitals. I too want to say the hell with it,

get myself exiled, take off into a Siberian snowdrift,
like a junkyard dog accustomed to
the vacant lots of the world,
but the days accumulate around me like glass baubles,
shattered by my body just stirring from sleep.
And I'm already on the bus heading to Queens College.

It's best that I keep building this ark.
I'll gather all the animals. I'll fill the vending machines
with American chocolate bars. I'll write letters to the mayor.
And the doves will return by the thousands
like every snowflake that fell the year Brodsky died
like me waking up in the early morning
to prepare my lecture and let the last dove go.

# AND I LEARNED OF FRIENDSHIP

I walked through an arcade of living ghosts
and she was there to greet me
at the breaking of the light. Giddy in Parisian street cafés,
my long eyelashes and her lips
wet and heavy with sugar.
I plumbed the skeleton of my heart, dumb and shy
with grief, and she collected
its little white bones and lit them like a lantern.
She asked to hear me sing,
so that the starlings would wake up tomorrow morning
to assume another shape in the sky.
And the Seine would keep the color of soiled linen
and we'd keep breaking into the world,
as if the future was as certain and simple
as laying down a tablecloth and opening a jar of marmalade.

And I sang. Of her pale belly—
a crabapple blossom of flesh rising and falling—
of her way of shaking her hands in praise of a small joy.
Of her red hair that sent Jacob up his ladder,
sea-captains on doomed voyages,
their dreams as distorted as the scales of an enormous fish.
In that the part of the world that had dreamt up
the most absurd gods, at yet another border,
I found her in the morning,
brewing a pot of coffee
and tearing a piece of bread in half.

# HOW I FELL IN LOVE WITH HENRY FORD

It didn't come on all at once like pneumonia;
the symptoms began
in starts and fits like the common cold.
At first I didn't notice. The tremble
in the throat, my flushed cheeks, bent over side-mirrors
to pick eyelashes out of my eyes.
Fragments of winter light
shattered like a champagne glass
over the city, receding in soft pink petal-tones.
A diadem grew over the carapaces
of chewed-up cars, piled on top of each other.
A crying tapered off the lots. The topless bar, with a nipple
and a high-heeled shoe
blinking over a gas station pump and a boarded-up motel—
a postcard from somewhere closer
than you'd imagine. I recognized it at once:
the will of god in the world,
Kant's plea that shipwrecked sailors
not be chased back into the sea. He dies a virgin.
Just like all the girls who move through dim halls,
as shiny as newly hatched stars.
Just like all the day laborers
who gather at a bus stop in Detroit.
Daybreak makes the sign
of the cross over them, their faces still soft with sleep.
They too will not be chased back into the sea.

# THE NEUTRAL ANGELS OF CANTO III

> "…and [they] were stung[.]"
> Dante

In the Ante-Inferno, the neutral angels
gather among those
who lived without praise and without blame.
Before the circles of hell even shudder open,
The Uncommitted are stranded on the riverbank.
They are unable to fly back to heaven
or cross Acheron
to enter the nested, inverted cathedrals.

Universally rejected,
they are envied by none of Cerberus'
three barking heads

nor by Paolo and Francesca in their passion
for learning the brief alphabet
of the body

nor by the suicides who cling
to their warm-blooded trees like a calf to its mother.

There, on that riverbank,
it is always the beginning of summer.
The cherry trees are in their first bloom.

These shades bend the world towards them.
They are where most of history happens.

When the firing squad raises their rifles
and border patrol agents
point a flashlight into the desert,

at the beginning and at the end of the war,
embargoes, auto-da-fé,

they stand apart, plant a garden,
dance at wedding receptions and dinner parties.

But a horsefly, goaded by eternity,
has already begun to hover over the potato salad.

# BIRDS

*for my kid sister*

I am moving up in the world my love.
I am a liturgy climbing the chambers of a small church
glowing among fireflies on a muddy roadside.
When I go out walking, I ride waves
of starlings that bend into the dusk
melting around me like a strawberry-flavored candy.
With the confidence of a backstreet boxer,
I have learned to let handsome strangers bandage my bruises,
search alleyways for my missing teeth,
pay me large sums of money for the show I put on.

Am I wrong, then, to want to take
with me our unwashed nights, a carton of expired milk,
a stone against which you tripped
and fell, neck first, on a broken glass bottle
and one or two cockroaches?
Or the occasional letter from the government
denying us something
we desperately need and that almost breaks my will.

Just as at a Jewish wedding one breaks glass
to remember, at the heights of love,
what was lost—the destruction
of the first temple—I want the wastes
and the old fears, so that I can reach out into the night,
crowded with washing boards
and piles of soiled laundry,
to arrive in the bungalow where we first met.

Your curls, knotted, clumped against your skin;
at first, your breathing frightened me,
it seemed to me an accordion pulled,
reluctantly, back and forth
through a tiny slit, when it was just
a birdsong making its way
in the dark to greet a new neighbor.

I learned to sing back to you, walk you to school,
feed you. And once,
using my entire paycheck
as a soda fountain girl in Roll-N-Roaster,
we rode horses on the beach.

And I learned that the terms of love
are always the same—
that of a bird that falls from a tree.
No matter what
stop what you are doing
to gather me, keep me,
and when the time comes, bury me.

# INTERLUDE FOR THE KING OF SPAIN,
## OR CONVERSATIONS WITH MY FATHER

### i. Polite Introductions

> "It's nothing more than a dignity;
> it's nothing visible you can take in your hands."
> Gogol, *The Diary of a Madman*

It's hard enough to walk past an open window
and not fling myself out of it
to win the acceptance of dogs exchanging greetings on street corners—
now you bring this up. There's something of a moralist
in you, a Bolshevik, a bank teller,

a Jew. Sorting notes long out of circulation.
Collecting coins from countries that no longer exist.
You can barely make out the wild animal
or the year faded in the copper—
a measure of human frailty that timestamps an ordinary heartbreak,
the beginning of a war,
the shocks sent backward in time

to the women who still stand in breadlines and outside jailhouses
for all of eternity. Now that it's happened once,
it's begun, the poisoning of the world.
A cloud hangs over St. Petersburg like a wet rag.
A street-sweeper crushes a moth under his broom.

Then something different:
A girl bathing in the Black Sea. When I first saw her,
bitten by the salt and the solitude
that real beauty imposes.
I could hardly keep myself from her, opening her colors
for everyone, like a real flower;
the naked sun sucked at her limbs, I at the jetties' lilt.

She was singing in Russian.
Black eyebrows, fat slinking over the muscle,
faithful to the hips and nipples
that beckoned like lighthouses.
Beset by suitors,
whereas I am the King of Spain. Pluto's only rival.
I opened the earth and she dropped in.
After all, children need their fathers.

You've become one of her travelling ghosts.
You've climbed into a glass bottle of memories that don't belong to you.
Sold for a discount at a junkyard sale in New Jersey.

Tell this story. The bones of your
great grandparents bleached in the sand dunes of Urumqi,
as I held her down
and watched her soul go limp in a poorly lit room.
A prophet of your choosing will return,
but you will have to make this right.
You'll have to clear my conscience, like sweeping
the leaves from a grave. Promise you'll visit
and cry over mine a little.
I must be a bad man. But you've turned out all right, haven't you?
A Bolshevik! A Uyghur! A Jew!
Bone of my bone.
Blood of my blood. This must be hard for you.
But isn't it good to live in the world? The world has so many people!
So many different kinds of animals!
Maybe some of them are good?

## ii. HOW TO SAVE THE MOON

> "…and it's all the doing of some barber
> who lives in Gorokhovaya Street."
> Gogol, *The Diary of a Madman*

In a druggist's glass bottle, carved into the ash-tree
of her departure, I've left instructions on how to save the moon.
That the moon needs saving is obvious.
She glows alone in the night sky,
as if it wished to be a victim of a highway robbery.

First, borrow a dropper of grease from a mechanic.
Sprinkle drops on the rim to loosen her from the pitch
of stars and slightly trembling nothingness.
If anyone starts asking questions
about why she hasn't been coming around,

replace the moon with a car tire or a stale loaf of bread.

Then, tie her down to a rail
in your garden like a stray dog or a birthday balloon.

And wait. Invite some friends for a game of cards.
Pour shots of vodka, help yourself
to a piece of pickled garlic, boil a head of cabbage.

Before you know it, you'll find yourself once again alone with the moon.

Her white eyes go black. You pickaxe her,
she looks so beautiful in that dress.

(Look, if you didn't want to get drafted into this war,
then you shouldn't have gotten yourself born.)

Toss her off a draw-bridge, throw her down a well.
Continue in this way until there's almost nothing left.
Not even a tooth to match an X-ray.

Although you've scattered her body like pieces of Lot's wife,
under a vacant sky, delight that you've saved her life.

## HOW MY FATHER BECAME A FAMOUS MATHEMATICIAN (OR WHY HE WASN'T ALL BAD)

> "…Procreation is an act as swift as the wave of Moses' wand;
> he sees nothing astounding in these miracles."
> Simone de Beauvoir

My father used to take me to the Central Branch of the Brooklyn Public Library when I was a little girl. I would sit beside him and he would tell me to be quiet. In Russia, he was a Professor of Mathematics at Moscow State University. In his student days, he was a boxer and a poet. After having his nose repeatedly broken by classmates yelling "*Zhyd*!", he wanted to learn both to break noses in return and to find metaphors for the taste of bloodied phlegm in the throat.

> In NYC, he drove a yellow taxi-cab to support our family. Desperate not to become academically irrelevant, and to keep publishing, he put his fists up; and he taught me to do the same. "The secret of a champion," he said, "is *learning to fall*. To take the hit. Just watch me."

At the red of a traffic light, he would resume working on his theorems. That's how he set to work, in frantic intervals blinkered by traffic lights. His driver's cubby was strewn with handwritten notes, tangled-up numbers and graphs, that flew in the guttering air, if a passenger asked him to roll down a window and unwittingly ruin a day's work. "God damn, Americans!" he would grumble. "Too lazy to walk a few blocks and leave me in peace!"

> He wouldn't take lunchbreaks. Everything he ate in a shift, which usually ran 15 hours, was smashed like baby food in glass bottles that also functioned as paperweights for crucial passages. And like a newborn, with his eyes half-closed, you can hear his strained breath as he ate. *Swish, shhhhhh.*

At the public library, we sat at any table we liked. I liked to pretend that we owned it, and with the magnanimity of philanthropists so embarrassed at our extraordinary wealth, we preferred to remain anonymous. From an early age, clearly, in matters of book learning, my arrogance was total.

> As far as I was concerned, we were the last adherents of Apollo's cult, ready to beat our chests at anyone opening a can of Coca-Cola or fiddling too long with a mechanical pencil. We were destined to answer the loftiest questions: What is a straight line? How do you know it won't eventually bend, mid-infinity, into some weird and inexplicable plane no one's ever heard of?

Desperate to stop this from happening, he would lay out his notes and pull books from the shelf, always the same books, every Saturday. Gauss and Reimann were impatient for him to touch their smooth pages. But the weekly miracle of Shabbos was that everyone in the public library waited for us; they seemed to stand still for a moment when we entered its oversized glass doors, raised their hats, closed their umbrellas.

> Overwhelmed by the feeling that he was cheating fate, my father would begin to waste time and find a rabbi or a librarian to argue with. I would look up at him, as he, laughing, interrupts the conversation to ask me, "Do you think I might still become a famous mathematician?" Without hesitation, every week, I would answer, "No."

## A SPIDERWEB GREW IN THE CORNER OF THE BEDROOM LIKE THE EIGHT EYES OF GOD

The most important thing to know
about my big brother
is that he broke his two front teeth
playing on a slide in a McDonald's
in Brooklyn in the mid 90s.
A light rain had made the metal
slick and flung him, face first,
into a life tinged with violence and insecurity,
the two wings of the dove of boyhood,
loveless and sad, no way
for anyone to search for dry land
or count the passing years.
Our parents said we couldn't afford
a 'cosmetic' dental repair.
That's how he learned what the destruction
of the body takes away from a person.
The pre-Socratics believed
that the soul was dispersed
through the physical body like a wind.
When you lose a piece of the body,
a little bit of the soul
departs with it, too.
I can't say for sure what those pieces
of tooth carried away with them.
But I hope he will find it again,
maybe in a leaf slowly falling from a tree
or a piece of bubblegum
that he accidentally swallows
and confronts, all at once, what he had lost.

## OUTSIDE THE BEDROOM WINDOW THE HONEYSUCKLE
## AND A FAMILY OF WHALES SWAM BY

Vaguely, in parts, like a ransom of light,
a line from a popular song
on the radio, I remember my little brother
had a pair of large brown eyes and long eyelashes.
How well liked he was by everyone.
That when he got to high school
girls would approach him in the hallways
to ask if they could be his girlfriend
and he always said yes. And that years later
he would confess to a breath in the dark,
"I think I love you but it's hard to tell."
We still have a lot in common.
We both died in a six car pile-up on the freeway.
Drifted across the U.S. on freight trains,
washing dishes and sweet-talking waitresses.
Ordered coffee at a diner and just watched the world go by.
Smoked cigarettes under a solitary streetlamp
and waited for someone we didn't think would return
and when they did
we turned away from everyone
to find an ending that makes sense.
Sometimes I imagine Jonah
sitting inside a whale. Maybe all this time
we've been sitting beside one another,
or maybe we were each
swallowed by our own respective whales.

# HOPE

*for Nadezhda Mandelstam*[2]

I am hope. I followed my spouse to the outskirts of the Russian empire.
I sat with him, delirious, in a cattle car,
as the North Star broke apart over the horizon.
Phoebus nursed its blue-grey fragments, dying of the cold
like ordinary men. I hear a Dardanian soldier,
a spear-thrust into his heart by Menelaus.
In the apotheosis of virtue and a boy's fear,
he screams my name. I collect poets
who throw themselves out of hospital windows in Voronezh.
I wheel a teacart in a large house, its clattering spoons
announce my arrival. I wait out the month.
I am unable to anticipate betrayal, his pale lips telling me to
GET THE FUCK OUT. I burn a tallow candle under wedding veils,
exchange wordless greetings with murderers
who search until the last minute for someone to change their minds.
Like an ice-locked lighthouse, I bloom in
the tundra, speckled with lichen trees, sedge, and the lithe
tracks of foxes, as the heavy leather boot of the night
cracks another rib. I am a snowed-in chrysalis,
a rolled-up manuscript sewn into the lining of a coat.
He almost forgot about me, lying on the barrack floor of a labor camp,
when the sun stood over him like a liberating army.
In a cut-out square of soot-bitten glass,
a family of cranes that will survive the winter were flying home.
So, he learns—apart from the spotted typhus
and the police agent sleeping peacefully in our Moscow apartment—
about his immortality:
that he is both an instantiation of a kind and Plato's original form,
a penniless Jew and the love of my life.

---

2    Author of the memoir *Hope against Hope* and spouse of Osip Mandelstam, a
Russian Jewish poet who dies in a labor camp in the winter of 1938. Nadezhda
translates as 'hope' from Russian.

A Uygyhur shepherd and his son pulled from a recovered family album.
The photograph omits their names or a date.

## WOULD YOU BELIEVE IT?

I am no longer sixteen. Impossible, really.
That I will not again crack
sunflower seeds on the salt-bitten boardwalk
as a pink gossamer slowly alights over the dripping void
of the early morning, carrying in
its belly the muted glory of another day on earth—
a bone that keeps washing ashore,
a child that insists on being born.

I won't talk through the night again
to junkies dozing to the clinking cowbell of withdrawal,
a pockmarked moonface hanging over us,
as if it were peeking inside a baby-carriage,
easing our loneliness; wherever I might go now,
you won't send police cruisers after me,
or watch with me seagulls throw up bits of a crab,
a shard of a dream that cuts the flesh when it releases you,
as you turn red in the face with worry over my future.

In the winter-agony of Coney Island,
where an old rabbi still blows his horn in a sad refrain—
and blue-grays settle over the blinking arcades
and wharves like a case of diphtheria—
I did not learn anything at all.
You were right, all my friends were idiots.

I will not pull back again a string over the rim of your guitar
and pick seaweed out of my hair, as if it were a lesson in cartography:
this is where my soul first flew to me,
this—where my knees turned in a little, the hands that came
to open them, kiss them. That I won't be kissed again for the first time
just about anywhere on my body.

Tomorrow morning in line at the welfare office,
you will exchange compliments with the secretary,
boredom silvering her eyes like a moonbeam from a Bulgakov novel,
forced to look at childhood photographs
of someone she does not love. And who really wants all this misery?
Even a poet eventually tires of it. The seagulls
will not return the last piece of your dream;
they will cry for you when you no longer need them to.

Maybe it only appears this way because god lives longer than we do
in the fat velvet ropes that droop
in between immigrant mothers waiting on a ration of eggs and milk
in the prayers we used to scatter
together at the marina like a crust of moldy bread.
We understand little of things' abrupt end—
and even less when they stubbornly continue—
and yet, it just so happens that whenever I stand in the enduring glow
of the Atlantic Ocean, I still believe that your life was the only thing that mattered.

# THE PART OF ME THAT'S A JEWISH POET

*in memory of my paternal grandmother Nelli Basevich (1917-2017)*

I.

The part of me that's a Jewish poet would like to sit
*shiva* for the rest of my life, raise a monument to Babi Yar
with the objects on my kitchen table: a book
of Italian poetry, a dirty spoon, an unopened bill from
the electric company. Like a spray of machine-gun fire,
a star-rise pierces the bluffs of St. Petersburg,
climbing the cathedrals that are swept up like roses
thrown on a stage. At the feet of ballerinas
pattering behind heavy curtains, dusk lowers its belly
into the dust of blown-out matchsticks
who still cling to their passports and implausible
interpretations of the Old Testament. In the bathtub,
I pour hot water over my limbs. I await a reprieve—
I dislodge a bullet from the Jewish part of my heart.

II.

*Beside a Lake*

The part of me that's a Jewish poet would like to
begin training for the Imperial Russian Ballet as soon as possible
to glide over the icy waters that spread in between larches
and smokestacks like raspberry marmalade.
Flying through the air, I'm confetti on New Year's Eve.
I'm Margarita on her broom. The wet eyes of pine needles
shake in the glass vale of the morning, snow falls from
thin, crooked branches. In the nighttime, everything
you loved floats above the city, folds in its leaves for Daphne
sprinting through the tangle, in case I too decide
to run for my life. But, the truth is, I am braver than anyone I
know or have read about. I have learned to move by watching ordinary objects:
the scaly fragments of bark, the migration
of butterflies, a piece of lace thrown over a sewing machine.

III.
Besides, the part of me that's a Jewish poet does not want refuge.
Under an overcast sky, for a living, I make passersby believe that anything
is possible—as you must have once believed, briefly.
The part of me that's a Jewish poet would like to believe, too.

*Over the bed in the ward, a small blue light announces a new soul.*[3]

Besides, I have a new routine. I sit on a park bench talking to myself.
I hold up to my face the scrawling behind a photograph
like a lantern and levitate into my future.
I read the pages of the Haggadah,
as if I were licking sprinkles off an ice cream cone.
I trade in sentiment as cheap and colorful as the flowers sold in train stations.
Tormented by nostalgia, as by a blackguard
and hungry seagulls, the part of me that's a Jewish poet
is lost in a parking lot in Detroit. I cannot fake it.
I leap without convincing anyone that I am a snowflake or a swan.

IV.
At least I am not in love with anybody. But, all the same,
the same part of me asks, aloud, with Amichai —
"Hey you there! (Do you love me?)" —
At least I am not waiting for it to rain frogs
and locusts, in spite of the shattering
of glass and bone, and the torch-lit marches, as midnight
strikes in America. And yet, I can still hear you
whisper in the night, "Yes, I love you. I love you. I love you."

*Exeunt*

The part of me that's a Jewish poet puts
her lips to a mezuzah and presses her mouth down hard.
I want him to feel my breath
through my teeth and spit and gaping nothings.
I make my presence known to the appropriate offices.
On a clear day in December,
a white rosette splits its body as it falls from the sky.
This is how it begins for us.

---

3   From Sylvia Plath, "The Surgeon At 2 A.M."

## OLD JOHN BROWN OF KANSAS

I know the will of god, I felt it move in the mountains
sink into the Swamp of the Swan
spin the barrel of my revolver and blow.

The snow drifted back to heaven, mixed with bits of brain
and bone. After the firefight,
my axe left a blood-print in the fields,

swung into their last breath. As I coaxed
the slavecatchers' dead white souls into the gravel,
the warm flesh of the state of Virginia shuddered under my hands.

This is how one builds a country.
This is how one praises god.
This is how one throws off the scent of the dogs.

Besides, I was never any good at raising farm animals.
I see, instead, souls that I cannot unsee.
I listen to what I cannot unhear:

the first draft of the Constitution, an unsayable hope,
the death of General Lee,
a voice that emerges from the blue-gray dark:

"Old John Brown of Kansas, are you a slaver
or a man of god? Can you see me?
*Who* am I when I'm in love? Asleep? Running for my life?"

I give you my weather-beaten bible,
a cache of rifles, two grown sons,
and my dream of America,

and, finally, I give you my body; like a candle in the mountains,
let it be a warm place to rest,
when the snow drifts back into heaven again.

# I WALK COME HOME AND WONDER HOW I GOT THERE

> "The way home we seek is that condition
> of man's being at home in the world."
> Ralph Ellison

I've arrived in this country before; in this very century,
maudlin cashier girls and ticket agents
minister to my physical body,
my need for clothes and toothpaste and a mailing address.

The miracle of walking home in the evening
to my assortment of things—a photograph
fallen behind a mirror, a minor constellation of notebooks,
a packet of flour that I've neglected,

now a bacchanalia of moths that my roommate
informs me originate from northern Europe
and have learned to consume the clothes that I can't afford,
the grain that I now can't use

and yet, it's a stroke of luck, really—as you know—
to have this little corner
of the earth: the traffic light bursts into my bedroom
like an overexcited child
before resuming its triumphant departure into the world,

the long, lapis exhalation of autumn
in the floorboards and the windowpanes, obscured by half-flowered
buds
and sparrows,
the used-up rag floating in the kitchen sink—

each proof that god was on our side all those years ago.
That I've been elected with a key
and a bedroom window—
with my own life that I can take into the city tomorrow

and station in the public library for hours,
writing apology letters to Sor Juana Inés dela Cruz
because I regularly abandon
my craft, as in later tonight, when I will go out dancing

in Brooklyn, and will be drunk and happy.
For it's no small matter to learn to apologize a little less
for one's own life. Crowded
into a train car or the hold of a decrepit cargo ship,

she was not indulging in life but belonged to it,
even as her limbs disarticulate under the hard muscle of the sea,
where she will remain alone in the dark, indefinitely.
One day, perhaps, that darkness too might speak,

maybe even go out dancing, and—who knows?—
get married and throw a lavish wedding party
because life will cast off its merchants, *all of them*,
who elect some into the world and un-elect others,
as if it were all the same, a small matter of detail.

When one looks from a sufficient distance,
it *is* hard to tell a human bone from a fish bone,
a girl from her screaming ghost,
and the earth from the undifferentiated darkness through which it floats.

## I SIT AT HOME AND WATCH TV ALL DAY

What if this is me at my best?
In the wastrels of blue light,
oblivious and happy,
my soul sprawls across the hours of the day
like a sunbather in flip flops
like a closed eyelid that just makes out
the shapes of the outside world float over me.
When every action has come
to its end, every emotion and mistake
the tracery of a lived life
that bends, forever, into a blue light,
a breath disappearing across a glass surface
like a record of everything you've done—
Aristotle thought happiness
was not a feeling,
but the space you leave behind after you're gone,
that you can only tell whether a person
was happy after they're dead.
He couldn't have known
that you can also tell when they're watching TV.

## THIS WAS A BAD IDEA

It was a bad idea: in the dripping faucet of the past,
humanity shoved into jet planes, peeking from behind hospital curtains,
standing around like cut flowers in a plastic bucket.

It was a bad idea for it, then, to mean so much.
An irremovable water stain.
A resolve that has left us unaccounted for.

But isn't it true that at least one person
somewhere is deciding that another matters,
loves her life, and suffers her body

like a conflagration of irises opening their mouths at once.
Mephistopheles thinks they are soft in the head,

when they are, in fact, imbeciles.
If you should happen across them, throw a glass of water

in their faces. Yet I am grateful to them for pulling
us from the void of our departure,
in which we didn't mean to go, much less be gone for so long.

When out of cowardice we fingered our own hearts
as if we were examining
a discounted vegetable at the supermarket,

we too took what did not belong to us: a bicycle, the iris-choked
arteries of Mnemosyne, a child's sleep,
this grief that was not entirely our own and was not entirely grief.

When the breaking water of our humanity broke,
returned, and multiplied like driftwood
and starfish, we too unintentionally trembled with light.

# THE HOLY CITY

It is hard to know the shape of a life
or of a city burning; a halo of gun powder
blows into the sea. The clear glass
of its nadir catches fire but nothing changes.
I search for the electrified chicken wires
among everyday objects,
a lipstick print on a wine glass,
a car speeding down a deserted street;
the road collapses behind it,
swallowed by a yawning chasm that looks
like another ordinary street.

Where can we find a new shore to wash up on?
This city, first dreamt by Cavafy, will always pursue us.

A star buries itself in the earth again, a castaway,
and I've been homesick for generations.
I have spent 6,000 years
wandering the earth, like a prehistoric river.

Even in an endless night, exile turns,
enveloped in the resin
of an ancient light, a branch that crowns
the godhead of the fleeing humanity.
After the clearing of a few leaves,
we drip back into ordinary space,
a star that hasn't yet been discovered in the night sky
that belongs to no constellation,
knows no nationality or space station.

All the same, it gets tiring to pick up
what you can of your belongings, to know that, in the end,
what belongs to you
is what you can carry in your hands. And if you're
lucky a field of white poppies will nod in the wind,

and someone will watch over your sleep.
What more should I paint on our amphora?
How can I describe a city being born?
That I can feel its fist opening in the earth
without disturbing the midtown traffic.
Often lying in bed at night,
the thought loosens the joints of my imagination.

And I think I can hear someone in the distance scream, "Hallelujah!"
A senator kissing a baby.

One day, lying in a magus straw bed,
pulled by a train of camels,
I will decide the worth of men.

But this is the desert you knew that I'd have to cross without you.

From this sand, I will shape a new people,
give them our language,
kiss their mouths and carry their children.
I'm giving them our golden age
and I can only hope that they deserve it.

Shake my hand, Reader,
it was good to meet you.

# AURORA

"Though should you see how great the services
I, but a woman, give when I preserve
at each new dawn the boundaries of night,
you'd judge some guerdon due."

Ovid, *Metamorphoses*

And for a guerdon I ask only
for the setting of bones, trampled by night's
inflamed cardia
and exposed to the neglect of the stars,
to bring my son, Memnon, back to life
to help me tell this story
because, Reader, speaking as one minor god
to another, as witnesses to this centrifuge of hurt and worry,
what we believe will be so,
and one book of poetry, one chance encounter,
one night of lovemaking could restore
the order of Thrace,
Bethlehem, and New York City.
So when you look up at me tomorrow morning
do not hesitate
to take off your clothes, to tell me what happened to you,
while you're at it, to make love to the world, too.

# EPILOGUE IN THREE FRAGMENTS

«На холмах Грузии лежит ночная мгла;
                Шумит Арагва предо мною.
Мне грустно и легко; печаль моя светла;
                Печаль моя полна тобою,
Тобой, одной тобой... Унынья моего
                Ничто не мучит, не тревожит,
И сердце вновь горит и любит - оттого,
                Что не любить оно не может.»

Alexander Pushkin[4]


"...We must begin at the beginning now—and this 'now' goes on
forever..."

G.W.F. Hegel


"...Out of the chaos would come bliss.
That, then, is loveliness..."

Dylan Thomas

---

4   "On the hills of Georgia, lies the night's gloom / The Aragva rolls at my feet / Grief-stricken but at ease, my sadness brightens / it brightens with thoughts of you, / You, only you...Nothing disturbs it, torments it; / And my heart burns again, and loves, / for not to love it is unfit." (Translated by the author)